# CONTENTS

I0190312

# WHEN FAVOR LOCATES YOU
## © 2016 Robert Andoh
### All Rights Reserved.

Rev. Robert Andoh
Pure Word Chapel (A/G)
P. O. Box 856, Sekondi
Ghana
Tel: +233 244 941 397 / +233 274 333 337
Email: *revbobandoh2@yahoo.com*

US CONTACT
3060 NW 70th Terrace
Miami, Florida 33147
Tel: +1 305 835 7421

**Published by:**
Quest Publications
6-176 Henry Street
Brantford, Ontario,
N3S 5C8
Canada
Website: *http://www.questpub.questforgod.org*
Email: *questpublications@outlook.com.*

Ordering Information:

Quantity sales. Special discounts are available on quantity purchases by corporations, associations, and others. For details, contact the publisher.


*Printed in the United States of America*


Because of the dynamic nature of the Internet, any web addresses or links contained in this book may have changed since publication and may no longer be valid.


Rev. Date: 30-Apr-16


ISBN-13: 978-0-9951872-0-7

*ISBN-10:* 0-9951872-0-7

# CHAPTER ONE

# THE MEANING OF FAVOR

The Longman dictionary defines 'favor' as something that one does for another in order to help them or be kind to them. Similarly, the Macmillan dictionary defines 'favor' as a behavior that helps someone and gives them an advantage in an unfair way. Considering what the word of God says in Psalms102—"Thou shall arise and have mercy on Zion, for it is the time to <u>favor</u> her, the set time is come"— 'favor' in the biblical sense is simply an act of kindness.

*I declare that from today people will show you much kindness because the set time for you to be favored has come, halleluiah! From today favor will locate you and people will show you kindness.*

Again, favor means to be liked; people will tell you that they don't seem to know why, but they just like you. You would be liked in spite of what people say about you.

Favor also means a time of approval, corresponding with how the Word Web explains favor—as an inclination to approve or a feeling of favorable regard towards a person.

*From today, favor will locate you and you will be approved where ever you go and in whatever you do. You will not be denied as you submit your application whether for employment, visa, loan for a business venture, or whatever you set out to do.*

Favor, yet implies being treated more than fairly. Sometimes you hear people make statements like, "we were not treated fairly". Well, favor transcends the realm of being treated fairly. To be favored is to have people on your side. Sometimes you find yourself in a situation and it appears everyone has deserted you, but when you find favor with God, He causes people to be on your side even when they don't want to do so. There are instances you might have legitimate reasons or grounds to bolster an idea or concept, yet you won't find anyone to listen to you. Oh, but when the favor of God is upon you, it propels people to listen and support you.

Favor also projects the idea of support or help. We are all products of help, right from the day we are born until the day we die. As long as you live, you will need help or support in cash or kind. Sometimes you look all around you, yet no help will be forth coming, but do remember Psalm 121:1 where like David, you need to say to yourself, "I will lift my eyes towards the hills from whence cometh my help." There is "help" for you and probably someone else will receive his/hers another point in time; but this time, in this season and hour, this help is specifically for you. Your help comes from the lord. Support is coming your way.

The plain truth is that we all need help at one time or the other. Fortunately for you favor will locate you, and when it does, you will receive help or support when you need it and even from quarters you least expected because God will be behind the scenes working on your behalf in order for you to manifest His favor on your life. This is a personal experience I want to share with you. I had the opportunity to preach during a conference in Atlanta on the theme *No More Impossibility.* On the first night, I talked about favor and the expectation was high. I was preparing the people for the next day of the conference as I told them I was going to preach on *Altars.* However, the next day the Holy Spirit said to me, 'just put aside your message and talk to them about miracles.' There was this professor who had been brought to the meeting, bed-ridden and had been in that condition for a long time. He was quite heavy since he couldn't move and was also in a diaper. There was this female pastor who also attended the meeting with her husband who was also a professor and apparently they knew the other professor and had invited him to the program. There was the willingness to attend the meeting, but coupled with the sick professor's wife's inability to handle him alone was the fact that they were staying quite a distance from the venue of the meeting. So the lady pastor and the husband who were coming from another city just wanted to be supportive, and thus, mobilized some lady ministers in the church to assist her at the professor's house. They helped clean him up, got him dressed and managed to get him into the wheel chair though one could see that he was uncomfortable in the chair. They were able to bring him to the meeting and sat him right in the front row. While I preached on miracles, I could see the professor was listening attentively to the word of God and this aroused his faith. When I was done preaching, I prayed for the sick and simply asked them to do what they couldn't do earlier without actually laying hands on them. All of a sudden, the professor pushed himself out of his wheelchair when the ushers quickly surrounded him to make sure that he did not fall, he just pushed them aside and he only continued to say that, "this is my time". This man received his healing that day. It was a Saturday, and on Sunday morning, as I sat at back of the church I saw someone open the door and the person was none other than the professor who was miraculously walking by himself, without any assistance whatsoever. The mind blowing part was that, as I sat at the back of the congregation, my eyes followed the professor as he walked in and sat in the front row. Then I realized that, not only had he been healed but within 48 hours, he had also reduced weight without going to the gym or undertaking any quick weight loss exercise. The same thing happened in the evening so instead of ending the program on Sunday, we had to end the conference on Monday night. *May favor locate you!*

When favor locates you, you find help. I am not fascinated by the miracle since I always see these miracles happening all the time but what fascinates me is the hearts of those women. The bible thus talks about the four men who carried their sick friend to Jesus but when they couldn't get access to Jesus because of the crowd, they climbed someone's building and let down the sick person right in front of Jesus. The bible says, when Jesus saw <u>their</u> faith, not the man's faith but the faith of the four friends, he healed the man. *May you have the faith of the four friends so that somebody would be able to walk into his/her destiny!*

The pastor would have been called to officiate the burial, if the family had waited for this man to die. But when you find favor, support will come and then help will come. Help is coming your way in Jesus' name.

When favor locates you, you enjoy certain privileges you would normally not have access to. Everyone goes through a lot of situations in life and some of these situations might be full of sorrows or joy, heartache or relief, anxiety or assurance. But encourage yourself in this, that if you have never been sorrowful, you will never know or value true joy. It is existence of one that makes you celebrate the other when you have it in your grasp.

Your days might be like a shadow, symbolizing decline so you seem withered like grass. When grass withers, it only means the life in it is gone and, like some people, just exists. This paints a picture in which people take no apparent notice of you; they virtually aren't affected when you come around or leave, yet you live. Now this is a situation that needs favor with immediate effect. Why? Well, you need to understand that favor brings transition and transformation, so have unshakable guarantee that you will live because things are going to change for the better. The bible says,

'Thou shall endure forever and thy remembrance unto all generations. Thou shall arise and have mercy upon Zion.'

Be sure and unwavering in your belief that God will have mercy on you. Mercy is so powerful. It is the reason why you are living. Share this moving story with me. In a certain hospital, it has been ascertained that everyday someone dies on 'this' particular bed at a particular time. So the hospital authorities conducted a lot of research to find out why someone, on that particular bed, dies at exactly 11:00pm every night. They had exhausted all possible reasons and they had just about given up when someone suggested that a security camera should be installed in the room to find why people kept dying in that particular bed at exactly 11:00pm. To their surprise they realized that the janitor who was supposed to mop the corridors of the hospital was responsible for that mishap. He was supposed to start work at 11:00pm and he normally plugged the socket of the vacuum cleaner in the room that contained the bed on which patients were dying every night at 11:00pm. Unfortunately, the janitor was innocently ignorant of the fact that, that bed was a life support bed and as such needed to be connected to a power source at all times. But this janitor would just unplug and cut the connection of life support to make way for the vacuum cleaner in order to enable him do his work; he did this without knowing that, it was at the expense of someone's life. It wasn't intentional but many people had died as result of this oversight. You may ask how favor and mercy played any role but let's remember this was detected just before another patient lost his or her life. I'm sure favor located that patient who would have been the next victim and it spoke for him/her. I want you to understand that mercy is a life support and whenever it is unplugged you simply die. That is why the bible says, c'it is of the Lord's mercies that we are not consumed, because his compassions fail not. They are new every morning: great is thy faithfulness.' (Lamentations 3:22). Mercy will sustain you until it locate you. There is, therefore, the need for you to understand that the devil cannot unplug the mercies of God and for that reason you will live, not die and will declare the mighty works of God.

# CHAPTER TWO

# WHEN YOU FIND FAVOR

To be favored means to be treated with favor and have special advantage. A special advantage is coming your way. When favor locates you, the situations are always treated with specialty. You would be treated differently.

Let me share another experience with you. I was at an embassy with a friend and I had the opportunity to chat with one of the top officials at the embassy. This really shocked my friend because the person I was chatting with was someone whose name sent shiver pills down the spines of many Ghanaians living in Italy in the 90s and early 2000s; but here we were having a good time together. So my friend said, "Papa this is really an achievement because people just tremble at the mere mention of this woman's name".

It is my prayer that, you will find grace. Favor is sometimes really not fair because it will say I have chosen this person and that's all there is to it.

God has already decided that you are his "own". Sometimes people look at you and think that you don't really deserve to be a child of God. This shouldn't worry you because you have been chosen. Favor has chosen you so you are going to have special advantages.

Let's take a look at the book of Ruth. The book of Ruth opens up the story of going to the town of Moab with his family to escape the famine in the town of Bethlehem, Judea and the bible indicates things turned sour for his family—the man died as well as his two sons, Mahlon and Chilion. They had been married to Orpah and the Ruth respectively. When God visited his people in Bethlehem, the woman (Elimelech's widow) decided to go back to her town. She tried convincing her daughters-in-law to go back to their people. They initially refused but later Orpah kissed her mother-in-law and returned to her people, which is why I've prepared a message titled "When you kiss, don't go". After kissing

11

Naomi, Orpah left and we never heard of her again. Judas also kissed Jesus and left and we never heard of him again but Ruth kissed and stayed on. They returned to Bethlehem. The people were excited to have Naomi back and welcomed by addressing her, "welcome Naomi" but she asked them to call her Mara. Take note of this: don't change your name because of the situation you might find yourself in and don't let temporary setbacks cause you to change your name. This is because temporary setbacks or inconveniences are meant for a permanent reconstruction in your life. So just endure, have the staying power and tenacity because if you didn't find Rachel—the reward of your labor and waiting— in the first seven years, you will definitely find her in the next seven years. So all you need is the staying power.

The bible continues with how Ruth decided to find something to do when they got to the land of Bethlehem and how her mother-in-law gave Ruth her blessings. Reading from the book of Ruth chapter 2:4 downwards it says,

"And behold, Boaz came from Bethlehem, and said unto the reapers, The Lord be with you.

And they answered him, The Lord bless thee. Then said Boaz unto his servant that was set over the reapers, Whose damsel is this?"

*From today, favor will locate you. You will be different among the damsels.*

When your set time is due, no matter how you appear, you will be selected and you will be different because favor would have located you.

(Ruth 2:6-8) "And the servant that was set over the reapers answered and said, It is the Moabitish damsel that came back with Naomi out of the country of Moab: And she said, I pray you, let me glean and gather after the reapers among the sheaves: so she came, and hath continued even from the morning until now, that she tarried a little in the house. Then said Boaz unto Ruth, Hearest thou not, my daughter? Go not to glean in another field, neither go from hence, but abide here fast by my maidens"

Drawing from the extract above, it's an undeniable truth that when favor locates you, you have security not only in your job but everything that concerns you. We are leaving in times when people, who have worked for years, go to work the next day and are fired without prior notice or anything to compensate for the years of tireless sacrifice. But let me announce to you that if you find favor, even when one thousand people are fired, you have no cause to fear because you will not be affected. *You might decide to resign on your own terms, but apart from that, you will never be fired.*

Boaz said to Ruth, don't go anywhere, stay right here.

(Ruth 2:9) "Let thine eyes be on the field that they do reap, and go thou after them: have I not charged the young men that they shall not touch thee?"

When you find favor, nobody can ever touch you again. You become the apple of God's eyes so if someone were to touch you, imagine who he'd be touching—the apple of God's eyes. You are the anointed of God and scripture says in Genesis 20:71 / 1 Chronicles 16:22,

"Touch not My anointed, and do My prophets no harm"

***Receive favor now, receive favor for today, and receive favor for all your days.*** Nobody can touch you because favor is all around you. Not only are you favored, you are also blessed. Following the story, the bible states that Ruth fell on her face and bowed down and said unto Boaz,

"Why have I found grace in thine eyes, that thou shouldest take knowledge of me, seeing I am a stranger? And Boaz answered and said unto her, It hath fully been shewed me, all that thou hast done unto thy mother in law since the death of thine husband: and how thou hast left thy father and thy mother, and the land of thy nativity, and art come unto a people which thou knewest not heretofore. The Lord recompense thy work, and a full reward be given thee of the Lord God of Israel, under whose wings thou art come to trust. (Ruth 2:10-12)

Sometimes when you do something for someone you consider it as nothing but the person rewards you in a very "big" way which makes you wonder why, but I want you to understand that,

that's the way favor works. Some of you are doing something you might deem too little and so might think no one is taking notice of it but one of these days, it will be declared fully. Any good thing done on this earth will not go to waste or unappreciated.

Share this testimony with me. A while ago I was holding a meeting at the Liberty Church in Accra and I remember there was a young man who will always turn up at my hotel, collect my clothes and wash them for me. He was a member of the church and he just decided to do that for me. So after the service we went back to the hotel together and I gave my clothes to him to be washed as usual. When he got home his wife asked him to whom the clothes belonged. When she was told that they were mine she decided to wash the clothes early in the morning before going to work. So early in the morning, she woke her husband asked for the second time whether the clothes were really mine and when she affirmed that they were mine, she made up her mind to wash the clothes with a scripture in mind. She said to herself, "God, when the woman with issue of blood touched the hem of Jesus' garments, she was made whole. Lord I am privileged to hold the clothes of your servant so turn things around in my life." She said, when she finished washing the clothes and was going to hang them dry them on the lines she stood by the drying lines and repeated her prayer.

She was a hairdresser and normally from Monday to Friday customers hardly come to set their hair. According to her, during the weekend just a hand full of people came to set their hair. The day she washed the clothes was a Tuesday and on that day in question she received quite a number of phone calls which were from her customers wanting to come and have their hair set. She goes on to say that at the salon, even though she had a baby strapped to her back which slowed her down, her customers were still willing to wait for their turn. She testifies that after that, she can say to the glory of God that things have never been the same since then. Nothing just happens.

I announce to you that, the little things you do will never go unrewarded, for the Bible assures that 'God is not unrighteous to forget your work of righteousness' (Hebrews 6:10), he will never forget that. For favor will one day bring to light all the little kindness you show to others that have been hidden and you will be overwhelmed by the returns. Nothing shall go to waste. I pray to God that all these things will come to light; on that day you'll sit yourself down and permit those streaks of joy flow down your cheeks as you ponder over how favor is smiling on you. ***Oh! Expect it at no later time, it is starting from NOW!***

A young man came to me and said to me, "Pastor, I am student at one of the universities and I would like you to grant me the privilege of praying for you anywhere and anytime you will be ministering. This is what I want to do". When God begins to bless such a person, people would ignorantly begin to say, 'we don't even know where he's coming from.' Well, they don't need to know where you're going—down the lanes of favor. Boaz said to Ruth, 'it has fully been declared to me all the things that you have done for Naomi and how you left your country to come and dwell in a foreign country with her.' When you are selfless, God will honor you. Then Ruth said,

"Let me find favour in thy sight, my lord; for that thou hast comforted me, and for that thou hast spoken friendly unto thine handmaid, though I be not like unto one of thine handmaidens." Ruth 2:13 (KJV)

When you find favor, you find comfort as well. Receive comfort for today. The psalmist says thy rod and thy staff, they comfort me. She said, 'thou hast spoken friendly unto thine handmaid, though I be not like unto one of thine handmaidens.' When you find favor, people speak to you in a friendly tone— soberly.

I once gave someone a call and the person on the receiving end answered the call using harsh tone, asking who it was that was calling. However, the person changed the tone immediately this person realized I was the one on the other side of the line. I then questioned the person's manner of answering the call, pointing out the fact that no one deserved to be spoken to that harshly.

*I pray that from today may no one be harsh towards you because YOU have found grace in the sight of God.*

Again, Boaz said to Ruth, 'at mealtime come thou hither, and eat of the bread, and dip thy morsel in the vinegar. Ruth 2: 14 reads, 'and she sat beside the reapers and she reached her parched corn and did eat and was sufficed.' So she left satisfied. From today, may you never be hungry. And when she was risen up to glean, Boaz commanded his young men saying, 'let her (referring to Ruth) glean ever among the sheaves reproach her not.'

When you find favor reproach is over. 'And let fall also some of the land on purpose for her and leave them that she may glean them and rebuke her not.' From today, no matter what you go through your hands will still be full. You will have something in your hand.

I was recently travelling to the States through Dubai. I was sitting beside some Muslim women and they were really nice people. For some strange reason, I felt a sharp pain in my ear; this usually happens to first time travelers. The women looked at me and with concern asked whether I was feeling pain in my ear, to which I said 'yes'. They told me the pain they also experienced on their first flight ever, and added that the antidote was to chew a gum. They quickly gave me a gum and true to their word, the pain eased as I chewed on it. Now, here are Muslims being a blessing unto me. It shouldn't surprise us when they seem to prosper, because by such acts, they activate the blessing in giving.

# CHAPTER THREE

# FACE TO FACE WITH FAVOR

I would like to share my personal testimony of how God's favour located me.

In 1990, I had a gentleman visiting the church for the very first time; I got to know he was a Ghanaian resident in Cote D'Ivoire with his family. After the service, we had a short interaction, during which time he told me that he'd greatly enjoyed the service, especially the message and inquired of me whether I would like to visit Cote D'Ivoire. I was excited to say the least, because it was an opportunity to step out of my home country Ghana for the very first time. So somewhere in June, we journeyed to Cote D'Ivoire. Thus, in June 1990, I enjoyed the new country and I was privileged to go with him the second time.

Again, in 1991, a good friend of mine, Bishop Prince Baah (Founder and President of

Christ Crusaders Ministry) was instrumental in my acquisition of a US visa; he took me to the American Embassy to acquire a visa to USA. I travelled to US in October, 1991 at nobody's invitation, yet I went ahead by faith and believing the scripture verse Ps 24:1;

"The earth is the LORD'S, and the fullness thereof; the world and they that dwell therein."

Arriving in the US, I was completely oblivious of where to go, not because I didn't know how to get to where I wanted to go, rather I had nowhere to go. Fortunately, a Ghanaian lady who was on the same flight to the US for the first time, had some family folks meeting her.

Before I left Ghana, my General Superintendent for A/G at the time, Rev. Asore and some other friends had handed me complimentary cards of people they knew. So the lady introduced me to her family and did talk of me being a pastor from Sekondi. They asked me where I was going, to which I indicated I didn't know; however, I showed them one of the complimentary cards that had a New Jersey address and pointed out that I intended to contact the person at the said address. They took a look at the card and estimated that the place I wanted to go wasn't too far from where we currently were. They were going back to Silver Spring, Maryland but they also had a friend from New York—Auntie Abena, a name I remember so well; she was more than willing to take me to the train station to look for the address I sought to find.

She volunteered to take me home and contact the people whose addresses were on the complimentary cards for any response, so they could possibly be directed to pick me up at their house. She was a Ghanaian with an African-American husband (who had been visiting the Larteh shrines in the Eastern region of Ghana for some time; he was well at home with Africa and consequently, the Ghanaian culture). She took me to her house as she promised; and this was Thursday, October 10th, 1991. When the man returned from work that day, the wife introduced me to him and narrated the circumstance within which she'd met me; how we were on the same flight and the encounter with her family who had come to welcome her at the airport. Also indicating how she, seeing I was stranded, had decided to extend a helping hand by bringing me home to rest and to contact the people whose complimentary card I had.

The husband was kind and quite welcoming because though tired from the day's work, he spent close to two hours on the phone, just trying to contact someone on the other end of the line to be of help to me. His efforts, sadly though, were futile as we didn't get through to anyone. Before he left the next morning, he offered to give me a ride to the train station so I could catch a train and go looking for the folks he'd been trying to contact. Considering my circumstance, however, I asked him if he'd be so kind to have me stay over for one more night, which he agreed. Throughout the day, I did nothing else than to fast and pray several hours seeking guidance and intervention from God.

The next morning was a Saturday, and once again the man was gracious enough to drive me from his home in New York to New Jersey, looking for the address on my complimentary card. We finally found it but there was no one there by the name stipulated on the card—it was heart breaking and devastating. He asked me what we should do and I handed him another card bearing the name of Rev. Adu Anto of Assemblies of God in New Jersey. He managed to locate the address and fortunately for us, he was home. A long discussion lasted between the pastor and the man while I waited: the pastor didn't know who I was but I found favour with him and he decided to keep me in his house for three nights since hadn't prepared for any guests.

On the second day, a complementary card giving to me by my general superintendent Rev. Dr. Asore which had the name of John Stembridge, the owner of Stembridge Furniture, at the 125th North East Street, Miami-Florida. I called the man and told him that his card was giving to me by Rev. Dr Asore who met him in a conference in Briton. There again favour spoke on my behalf and the man asked me to come over. I set off in an Antrack train, a very fast one at that, but the journey lasted thirty hours and fifteen minutes: departing on Thursday morning at nine O'clock and arriving on Friday afternoon at fifteen minutes past three. Those were days we had no cell phones, so I called the man from a toll booth. I thank God my arrival was in the afternoon. For I do think about how I would have managed if my arrival was at dawn; but because the steps of the righteous are ordered by the Lord, He had it all worked out perfectly in his own plans. Mr Stembridge asked the Haitian gentleman to pick me up from the train station to his store. Mr Stembridge had a small Jewish fellowship and asked me to speak to the members of the fellowship that evening after which we went to a restaurant; that was my first time of stepping into an international restaurant. I have actually forgotten what I ate that night but I do remember the dessert I ate that night, it was Ki lime pie (and I will never forget it my first desert in my whole life. Stembridge then took me to the Howard Johnson hotel and paid for a night's stay, and informed me that he'd be out of town the next morning—beloved, that was the beginning of my nightmare. He did give me two complimentary cards of two Spanish pastors whom he suggested I could contact to possibly secure the opportunity to preach the gospel, which I'd indicated was the prime reason for my traveling. That night, I couldn't sleep for fear had gripped my heart, preying on the uncertainty that loomed for the coming day. I was in total oblivion concerning where I was going after check out, so I only prayed and prayed, and cried and cried, and prayed and prayed, and cried and prayed the more…until morning. The thought and fear of the unknown path that awaited me drenched my eyes with tears, and as tears continued to stream down my face, I heard the sound of praise and worship going up before the throne. With an eager heart, I stepped out to find where this was happening, only to realize that the door opposite my room opens to the conference hall. There was a group of ministers who had formed a fellowship which I later got to know was called Baruch Christian fellowship that convened meetings at the Howard Johnson hotel on the third Saturday of every month.

There is absolutely no doubt that God had arranged events in such a way that I had to leave New Jersey the Thursday morning, arrive on Friday afternoon only to meet this group of ministers on the third Saturday in the very hotel where I spent the night. I went in to join them in fellowship, and they could see that I'd been crying for a long time. I was given the opportunity to introduce myself and say a few words and after that, I found favour with virtually everyone there. When the service ended, most of them interacted with me briefly, hugged me and left. I prayed to the Lord, 'I need something more than a hug...' I needed an intervention by the hand of God. As most people took leave of the room, there remained about four ladies and a gentleman by name was Billy Hester. He approached me and asked where I was heading, and knowing what I knew, I opened up with brokenness of heart and told him that I'd come to look for an opportunity to preach the gospel; that I had no place to stay, nor did I have money could I stay at the hotel. He then walked over and spoke to his wife, Martha Hester, to her awhile and they agreed to have me over at their house. In my interaction with the couple, I found out that they both decided not to attend the fellowship that particular weekend but that Saturday morning, the wife prompted Hester telling him that they needed to get dressed and get on to the fellowship. Hester wondered at the wife's change of mind because he remembered they had taken a decision not to attend; nonetheless, he indicated that he felt a prompting to get up, get dressed and go ahead with the wife. As we got to their home, they concluded that God wanted them there at that particular time just to help me out.

We then proceeded to called one of the Spanish pastors, Miguel Escoba, who offered to give e his pulpit on the Sunday, which happened to be my first international platform and, believe me, I preached. Graciously, God confirmed his word with supernatural manifestations; people were all over the floor under the power of God without a touch from anybody. When we got home after close of service, Hester, who had just heard me preach for the first time, picked his phone and started making calls to pastors that he knew. He had a very good relationship with a lot of pastors, whom he talked to about an African brother he and the wife had met stranded in a hotel, whom they were hosting in their home, and how my ministry had been a blessing to them and his church. There and then, I had sixteen invitations within four weeks. Most of the churches I preached in, in south Florida, Miami specifically, would make their church van available and ask the members to come support me in my next meeting. In one of the churches in Opa-Locka, called Christ Crusaders Ministries, I encountered

the head pastor who was then, in the person of
Pastor Juanita Mincey. After my ministry in that
church, Pastor Mincey said to me, "Bro Robert, we
want you to know that our church mother has a great
desire to see Africa before she dies, yet we have no
contact in Africa. Immediately you stepped into this
house of God, God spoke to my heart,' I've brought
my servant as my answer to your prayers'". Pastor
Mincey the decided to come to Africa first before
deciding whether or not it was worth bringing the
old woman to fulfil her dream. I'd then found favor
with Pastor Mincey who had accepted me as a son.
We fixed a date and she visited Ghana and I quite
remember we had just returned from our first day
tour of Sekondi and as we had dinner, she said,
'I noticed the people here need some vitamins'. I
asked why she thought so and she indicated that
she observed that the people were very slow. Then
I explained to my mum that it wasn't a vitamin
deficiency, however, they had no place to go and so
they didn't see the need to rash. On the second day
of our tour, we passed by the Sekondi fishing harbor
where I had carried fish al my youthful life, just to let
her appreciate the sort of background from which I'd

travelled to the US. On our way back, we passed by a huge building which used t be a liquor factory—Brennya Distillary Company, which had been shut down and was up for sale. I'd never asked for the price of a property or a stretch of land, never in my life because I knew it wasn't time yet; but something urged me on, which I believe was the spirit of God and I said, 'I wish I had the money to buy this line of buildings'. Immediately my mum, Pastor Mincey, heard that she said, 'son, if that is what you want, we would help you to get it'. I was shocked to the spine. Now, this wasn't a mere property to own, not a shoe, not a shirt, nor food—this is a fleet of building properties.

On her back to the USA, we stopped by the Trust Bank, currently Ecobank, which was on the *Kojo Thompson* road in Accra and she opened a foreign account for me and promised she was going to send me some money to help me buy the property. She later called me, after her safe arrival in the United States, and asked me to go to the bank and check. My spiritual mum had sent thousands of US dollars and I'd gone to see Uniliever, who owned the property to express my interest in purchasing the building. I didn't look serious to the staff of the Uniliever Company because I did not look nor carry the aura of a person who had the purchasing power to own such a line of properties. In spite of that, I did go to the company with the money which I'd redrawn at the bank prior, with Reverend Ernest Kwadwo Agyei, who is the current pastor of His Excellency the President of the fourth Republic of Ghana. We withdrew and changed the money, which we put into two *"may3 ay3 yie"* bags *(making-strides-to-prosper bags);* then we went ahead to pay for the properties.

On the day we entered the bank and my two eyes beheld dollars acquainted with my name in bank language, I ended my long relationship with poverty. Suddenly, I was the owner of an enviable line of assets—from a poor humble background, never asked for the price of the smallest stretch of land, but now my name appears in the ownership blanks of properties. It is really amazing what favor can do in a minute, for hard work alone couldn't have achieved such, not even in a century.

How I pray that everyone reading this book will reach out in faith and believe what the psalmist is saying in Ps 102:13 that,

> "Thou shalt arise, and have mercy upon Zion: for the time to favour her, yea, the set time, is come."

My encounter with Pastor Mincey opened up my ministry in Africa and in the US to the mayor of Opa Locka at the time, who honored me with a citation and a key to the city.

We bought the building and then Ps. Juanita Mincey and the church finally agreed to come to Africa with their church mother to fulfil her longing to see Africa before passing into glory. Eventually, they did come to Africa, and in the entourage that accompanied Ps. Mincey was her niece, Dr. Patricia Seabrooks—a lady who was a top ranked US official, specialized in military clinics. Dr. Seabrooks had a heart for needy people and was in the service of offering free medical care for needy people in Haiti. She saw a good avenue to introduce this free medical care in Sekondi by using our church to house a temporal clinic for two weeks. It was truly impactful because several hundreds of people thronged the church premise to receive free medical care.

Dr. Seabrooks then invited a friend by name Dr. Leda Mcenry who was then the Dean of the School of Nursing in University of Massachusetts, to come over to Sekondi, Ghana, to witness what she had started. In the course of time, the school of Nursing in the University of Massachusetts took over the project and run the free health care twice a year for about fifteen years; other Universities like the Presbyterian University Hospital, the Medical University of South Carolina, Clemson University, to name a few, came under the gracious umbrella of this impactful mission.

Eventually, the Dean of Babson College also came into the scene to estimate what contribution they could render in the business community. Babson College worked with our Secondary Schools that offer business courses, and educated several other thousands of students with entrepreneurial and leadership skills up unit 1 2014. In 2015, Wheaton College in Massachusetts took over the business branch of the project, still under the inspiring leadership of Dr. Dennis Hannon, who had advanced from being Dean at Babson College to be President in Wheaton College University in Massachusetts. Currently the medical mission is progressing under the leadership of Dr. Morton, who took over from Dr. Leda McKenry when she retired.

These connections opened the door for me to preach to the US military in 1996 in Yeung-Sung, South Korea— a favor only the heavens can bestow. Just about ten years ago, my city celebrated its centenary; and by virtue of these projects that I oversaw in the community, I was privileged to be among the few that the community honored with a citation and a plaque for my contribution towards the socio-economic development of the city.

To God be all the glory, for the great things He has done. In spite of these secular favors, I have been preaching the gospel and crisscrossing the continents more than ever—to Jehovah alone be the glory.

As it was said to Naphtali,

"Satisfied with favor, possess thou from the south and the west…"

So I speak to everyone who may not bear the name Naphtali, but might be going through the implication of the name in struggle,

*May every struggle of your life come to a perpetual end; may favor step in. May you catch the revelation that this is the set time for God's favor. It's your time for favor, for favor ends all the struggles and puts you in the flow of divine possessions.*

*I prophecy that the Lord will show you great favor and cause favor to locate your dwellings, end all your struggle and begin your journey to the zenith of life where you belong. For it is said that you'll be above and not beneath. You'll be the head and not the tail. The Lord bless you as you encounter favor, in Jesus' mighty name.*

*May you and your entire household, may you and your bloodline receive the God kind of favor that will catapult you to the heights you have always dreamed. I declare to your spirit to never give up for destiny*

*helpers are just about knocking on your door. It's a new day; it's a new season, it's a new season.*

*You are called among the blessed. You'll be too blessed to be stressed. In Jesus' name, Amen!!*

# About the Author

**Rev. Robert Andoh** is the Lead Pastor of Pure Word Chapel (Assemblies of God) in Sekondi, Ghana. Called, ordained and commissioned into the Apostolic and Teaching ministries. He travels extensively around the world as a highly sought after conference, seminar and revival speaker. He features regularly with Bishop Charles Agyin-Asare in his citywide crusades and schools of ministry conducted in several nations of the world.

He is also the C.E.O. of the International Missions Foundation, a humanitarian mission, which in collaboration with his foreign partners, has given medical and business assistance to over 50,000 needy people in Ghana. A highly resourceful person, Rev. Andoh for the past fourteen (14) years has been the annual outreach coordinator in Ghana for some universities in the USA.

His messages based on the pure Word of God and backed by the power of the Holy Ghost are always followed by the practical demonstrations of the miraculous, thus challenging and changing his audiences to accepting without controversy, the Lordship of Jesus Christ.

Rev. Robert Andoh is married to Augustina with four children.

www.ingramcontent.com/pod-product-compliance
Lightning Source LLC
Chambersburg PA
CBHW060042040426
42331CB00032B/2241